WHEN YOU DON'T KNOW

WHAT TO
SAY

*How to Help Your
Grieving Friends*

SECOND EDITION

HAROLD IVAN SMITH

BEACON HILL PRESS
OF KANSAS CITY

Copyright 2006, 2012
By Harold Ivan Smith and
Beacon Hill Press of Kansas City

ISBN 978-0-8341-2799-9

Printed in the
United States of America

Cover Design: Lindsey Rohner
Inside Design: Sharon Page

Library of Congress Cataloging-in-Publication Data

Smith, Harold Ivan, 1947-
    When you don't know what to say : how to help your grieving friends /
Harold Ivan Smith. — 2nd ed.
        p. cm.
    Includes bibliographical references (p.   ).
    ISBN 978-0-8341-2799-9 (pbk.)
    1. Church work with the bereaved. 2. Bereavement—Religious
aspects—Christianity. I. Title.
    BV4330.S577 2012
    248.8'66—dc23

                                                    2011039096

10 9 8 7 6 5 4 3 2 1

DEDICATION

"Let's hear it for the ladies of the church . . ."
(these days "the folks" from the church)
who cook and bake and clean and show up.
Who care and comfort.

They come not with answers and solutions
but with the gift of presence.
They make a difference.

There are no banquets in their honor, no plaques,
no certificates of appreciation,
but they bring a smile to God's face.
Thank you.

contents

A Grief Sharer's Prayer

Lord, take me where you want me to go;
Let me meet whom you want me to meet;
Tell me what you want me to say, and
Keep me from getting in your way!

Father Mychal Judge°
Death Certificate Number One, Ground Zero

°New York City Fire Department chaplain who died at Ground Zero September 11, 2001. While administering last rites to a critically injured person, Judge removed his fire helmet so the dying person could see his face. He was struck in the head by a flying object. Firemen carried him to their fire hall.

Blessed are the helpers who are uniquely themselves.

Blessed are the helpers who weigh words carefully and avoid clichés and platitudes.

Blessed are the helpers who give grievers permission to feel pain and to cry and to ask questions.

Blessed are the helpers who willingly receive the lament and the stories of the bereaving.

Blessed are the helpers whose hands are always ready to applaud the baby steps of the bereaving.

Blessed are the helpers who show up and anticipate what needs to be done.

Blessed are the helpers who send cards and notes—and keep on sending them.

Blessed are the helpers who show love tangibly by sending flowers or donating to designated charities.

Blessed are the helpers who attend the rituals.

Blessed are the helpers who pray.

Blessed are helpers who make sure grievers eat and who eat with grievers.

Blessed are helpers who familiarize themselves with what it means to grieve.

Blessed are the helpers who can confidently recommend skilled counselors and support groups and books.

Blessed are the helpers who visit cemeteries.

Blessed are the helpers who remember anniversaries.

Blessed are the helpers who celebrate Memorial Day.

Blessed are the helpers who notice children.

Blessed are the grief sharers who give their grief a voice.

Blessed are the helpers who remember that grief sharing is vital kingdom work.

PART 1

RESPONDING
WITH YOUR
presence

WISE WORDS FOR LOANING

"We can walk up to any reality—no matter what it is—
knowing that God is already there waiting to
anoint it with the oil of his blessing."

—Carolyn Lunn

CHAPTER 1

COMPANIONS IN THE PAIN

At some of the darkest moments of my life,
some people I thought of as friends deserted me—
some because they cared about me and it hurt them to see me
in pain; others because I reminded them of their own
vulnerability, and that was more than they could handle.
But real friends overcame their discomfort and came to sit
with me. If they had no words to make me feel better,
they sat in silence (much better than saying,
"You'll get over it," or "It's not so bad;
others have it worse"), and I loved them for it.

—Harold Kushner, *Living a Life That Matters*, 123-24

We learn what to say, in part, by listening to what is being
said. If we let the person tell us where he or she is,
we will soon learn how best to respond.

—Thomas Oden, *Pastoral Theology*, 299

Blessed are those who mourn,
For they will be comforted.

—Matt. 5:4

Eight-year-old Becky was late getting home from her friend Christine's house. Again, and even though her father had warned, "Becky, the next time you're late, you're going to be in big trouble."

When Becky walked in, her father demanded, "I told you to be home at five! What do you have to say for yourself?"

"Well," Becky began, "I was playing with Christina, and she dropped her doll and broke it . . ."

The father interrupted: "And I suppose you were helping her pick up the pieces."

"Oh, no, Daddy. I was helping her cry."

This old story captures the role of the helpers in responding to the bereaving. To be bereaved is to be *reaved*. *Reave* is a wonderful old English word that means to break, to plunder, to rob, to tear apart, or to deprive one of something. Thus, the griever can say, "I am *reaved*" and be precise.

Many bereaved do believe their world has been torn apart, and in reality it has been forever changed.

Many bereaved believe their lives, memories, and futures have been plundered.

Many bereaved believe they and their families have been torn apart.

Many bereaved, as they age, believe they have been robbed of emotional companions. We can replace lost objects, but we can't replace children, spouses, siblings, friends, and a shared future with them.

The grief sharer's role is to help them grieve.

Penelope Wilcock illustrated: "Our response to the helplessness of others is to take rescuing action, to be the cavalry coming over the hill" (*Spiritual Care of Dying and Bereaved People,* 4).

How can we be the cavalry for someone going through grief?

First of all, grief sharers must ask, "Am I willing to be changed by this experience?" Gerald Sittser, whose wife, mother, and daughter were killed in an automobile crash, writes that "Good comfort requires empathy, forces adjustments, and sometimes mandates huge sacrifices. Comforters must be prepared to let the pain of another become their own and so let it transform them. They will never be the same again after that decision" (Gerald Sittser, *A Grace Disguised,* 159).

In Judaism, temple or synagogue members who care for the body, especially the ritual washing, after a death are called the *Chevra Kadisha,* or "Holy Society." These people are always "on call," because most Jews are buried within 24 hours.

As a Christian, you, too, can be "on call" to opportunities for intentional sharing. Through your presence, you can make a difference—even when you don't know what to say or do.

No one should have to walk alone through the valley of death's shadow. "When Job's three friends, Eliphaz the Temanite, Bildad the Shuhite, and Zopar the Naamathite, heard about all the troubles that had come upon him, they set out from their homes and met together by agreement to go and sympathize with him and comfort him" (Job 2:11).

Like Job's friends, we can walk *with* the bereaved if we see and seize the opportunities for grief sharing.

A COMPANION ON THE PATH

Two men sat eating breakfast one morning in 1871. One had been lost in the jungles of Africa for five years until Henry Stanley, a reporter for the *New York Herald*, found him with the now-famous words "Doctor Livingstone, I presume."

The men developed an intense friendship, but now it was time for Stanley to return to New York. As they finished their meal, Stanley broke the silence: "And now we must part. There is no help for it. Good-bye."

"Oh, I am coming with you a little way," Livingstone said. "I must see you off on the road."

As they walked, finally Stanley stopped and said, "Now, my dear doctor, the best of friends must part.

You have come far enough; let me beg you to turn back."

Livingstone studied his friend and replied, "You have done what few men could do—far better than some great travelers I know. And I am grateful to you for what you have done for me" (George Seaver, *David Livingstone: His Life and Letters*, 595-96).

Like Livingstone with Stanley, your task as a grief sharer is to see the bereaving "off on the road." You cannot do your friend's grief for them. You are not called to supervise or critique that person's grief. You are, however, called to *witness* this person's courageous efforts to come to terms with loss. Like a cheerleader on the sideline during critical points in the game, you call encouragement to those on the field. By your gifts of care, time, and silence, you, too, may eventually hear, "You have done what few . . . could do. . . . I am grateful to you for what you have done."

Grief care is an opportunity to be a companion on the path, a companion in the rough times, a companion for the moment when hope lights the way—and a companion in the daily struggle of grieving. One of the most significant things you can ever do is to be a grief companion.

You may protest—"But I don't know what to say." You are not the first person to utter those words. When God tapped Moses to lead the Israelites, he protested:

"O Lord, I have never been eloquent, neither in the past nor since you have spoken to your servant. I am slow of speech and tongue" (Exod. 4:10).

The Lord responded to Moses as I think he would respond to decliners today, "Now go; I will help you speak and will teach you what to say" (v. 12).

That promised assistance should have been enough to overcome Moses' hesitation, but it wasn't.

Moses pleaded, "O Lord, please send someone else to do it" (v. 13).

Someone else. We're so good at passing the buck.

"Oh, Ruth can do it. She's so organized. Or Bill—he always knows just what to say. Or how about Ann? She's a stay-at-home mom and has plenty of time. How about Carl and Mabel? They're retired. It would give them something to do."

The Sovereign of the universe invites you to participate. You'll miss out if you cling to "I don't know what to say."

In the aftermath of the September 11, 2001, terrorist attacks in New York City and Washington, D.C., people naturally asked, "Where was God?"

In a grief's weary, dreary days, God shows up through his field reps, people such as you. These individuals don't necessarily know what to say or what to do. But they show up, sit down, and stay awhile.

In *The Art of Being a Healing Presence* James Miller reminds us, "There are three things you can do to help someone. The first is to listen. The second is to listen. The third is to listen some more" (39).

Grief sharers always look for an opportunity to actively care. You can never "fix" an individual's grief, but you can wash the sink full of dishes, listen to him or her talk, take his or her kids to the park. You can never "fix" an individual's grief, but you can visit the cemetery with him or her.

Grief sharing is not about fixing—it's about showing up. Coming alongside. Being interruptible. "Hanging out" with the bereaving. In the words of World War II veterans, "present and reporting for duty."

The grief path is not a brief path. It's a marathon, not a sprint. Because of their own apprenticeship on the path, grief sharers have learned the accuracy of Theresa Huntley's assessment—"Although the grief that you carry remains with you forever, ideally it will become a part of—rather than all of—your life" (*When Your Child Dies*, 47).

The issue is not "getting over" grief or "moving on" (or any of the other clichés we have created to signal our impatience with grief). The issue is what the bereaving will do *with* their grief. And who will share their grief with them? Who will be with them on the most difficult parts of the path?

In my neighborhood is an impressive private school for boys that is a result of a deep grief. In 1953, six-year-old Bobby Greenlease was kidnapped and murdered. Many parents would have turned bitter, but Virginia Greenlease and her husband poured themselves and their financial resources into Rockhurst High School and Rockhurst University, donating the land that became the high school campus. Over the years, Mrs. Greenlease paid the tuition for many boys.

Why were the Greenleases so generous? They never forgot the round-the-clock kindness of Rockhurst's Jesuit priests who became grief sharers with the distraught family. Virginia Greenlease lived 48 years after the incident, balancing the memories of her son's kidnapping with memories of a great high school and the boys who "did well" (Tim Higgins, "Virginia Greenlease, Benefactor of Rockhurst Schools, Is Dead at 91," B1).

Like Becky in the opening story, you can help people cry. You can help people lament and laugh. Remember in reality, in time, the positions will be switched, and those who have received comfort and condolences will be the comforters. Sooner or later, everyone walks a grief path. Will that path be yours alone, or will it be shared?

CHAPTER 2

GrIef SHarInG

*Here's what I've learned about grief: it's not linear,
it's not predictable. It's anything but smooth and
self-contained. Someone did us all a grave injustice
by implying that mourning has a
distinct beginning, middle, and end.*

—Hope Edelman in *Motherless Daughters*, 5

*Do not be far from me, for trouble is near
and there is no one to help.*

—Ps. 22:11

One of the darkest moments in Christianity occurred as Jesus faced crucifixion. The description of Jesus' arrest is followed by sobering words that many grievers can appreciate: "Then everyone deserted him and fled" (Mark 14:50). Everyone. The sleeping disciples in Gethsemane have been criticized abundantly, but the "sprinters" have gotten off without much comment. One young man was so eager to get away that he "fled naked, leaving his garment behind" (v. 52).

Many bereaved people have experienced someone "dropping off" a casserole and leaving in a matter of seconds. Others "drop by" but never take off their coat or sit down. "Can't stay—just wanted to see how you're doing," they say. (But if you don't stay, how can you hear how they're doing?)

Historically, Christians have not sprinted away in the face of pain. Early believers not only cared for the grieving but also buried the dead. Christians graciously washed and laid out the body, wove shrouds, gathered flowers, dug the grave, carried the corpse, and fed the bereaved; they also gathered on the third, ninth, and fortieth day after the death to pray.

Many do not know, given our understanding of cultural history, that all the responsibilities of dying care, death care, and grief care were once provided by church folk, friends, and neighbors. There were no professionals to offer such services.

Brent Russell calls Joseph of Arimathaea "the patron saint of funeral directors" (56, 58). Although a secret disciple, while the others were fleeing, Joseph gutsily approached Pilate and asked for Jesus' body (Matt. 28). (No member of the family or the inner circle was attending to such details.) Roman law stipulated that only family members could request the body from civil authorities. Moreover, in the case of a convicted criminal, the body was to decompose at the site of the crucifixion. To the Romans, Jesus was a traitor. So a friend of a traitor naturally arouses suspicion.

Imagine such courage in getting involved to see that Jesus was buried properly, and before the start of the Jewish Sabbath.

Anyone handling or touching a corpse made himself ritually unclean for worship observance (Lev. 21:1-12; Num. 19:10-13). In fact, the high priest could not enter a place where there was a dead body (see Lev. 21:11). Thus, funeral responsibilities were assumed by lay individuals who "undertook" the responsibilities to prepare the dead for burial while pastors developed a funeral sermon. Over time this gave birth to the term *undertaker.*

In the last 50 years in North America, the funeral director's role has evolved from preparing and burying the dead to coordinating the funeral, consoling bereaved families and friends, and blending the roles of counselor, confidant, detail manager, and seller of goods and services. A whole range of associated businesses now offer goods and services once supplied by volunteers: beauticians, cemeterians, florists, and even in some settings, pallbearers.

This ministry of showing caring after a death was so significant that James concluded, "Religion that God our Father accepts as pure and faultless is this: to look after orphans and widows in their distress and to keep oneself from being polluted by the world" (1:27).

In an era before Social Security, pensions, and life insurance, a death often caused great distress; some women had to turn to prostitution to survive. The societal financial net for widows and orphans in our era has allowed most of us to ignore the implications of this passage and, as a result, to miss the blessing for such servanthood. No wonder we moan, "I don't know what to do."

Simeon J. Mastlin feels the motivating element in Judaism for good works is Ps. 24:1—"The earth is the Lord's, and everything in it." He says, "Since everything belongs to God, we are merely the stewards of His infinite blessings, and it is, therefore, incumbent upon us—i.e., it is a mitzvah [good deed]—to share His substance with others who are in need" (*Gates of Mitzvah: A Guide to the Jewish Life Cycle*, 122).

We are the conduits through which God makes his blessings known. The underpinning for a mitzvah, or good deed, is found in Lev. 19:9-10. This scripture instructed landowners to leave the edges of their fields unharvested so that the poor, the widowed, and the orphans could gather this food and survive. People could not ignore the widowed or orphaned in ancient biblical culture; their survival depended on compassionate care.

When a widow sought Elisha's intervention to prevent creditors from seizing her two sons to settle her husband's debts, the prophet did not send her to a social worker. After Elisha inventoried her resources (a little oil), he instructed, "Go around and ask all your neighbors for empty jars. Don't ask for just a few" (2 Kings 4:3).

Then, as Elisha prayed, the family poured the oil, filling the jars. When they ran out of jars, the oil stopped flowing. Elisha told the widow to sell the oil and liquidate the debt, promising, "You and your sons can live on what is left" (v. 7), which sounds like "and they all lived happily ever after."

Perhaps no one neighbor could have solved the financial distress. But together they contributed vessels for the miracle. The widow was rescued by a community response.

Today many grievers fall through the cracks, sometimes overlooked in an era of frantic busyness. Jesus' words can be troubling:

I was hungry and you gave me something to eat.

I was thirsty and you gave me something to drink.

I was a stranger and you took me in.

I needed clothes and you clothed me.

I was sick and you looked after me.

I was in prison and you came to visit me (Matt. 25:35-36).

Admittedly, this passage does not include "I was grieving and you . . ." but it does not require a leap of faith to sense this in the spirit of Jesus' words.

The righteous sputtered, "Lord, when did we see you hungry . . . or thirsty . . . a stranger . . . needing clothes . . . sick or in prison . . . ?" (vv. 37-39). If Jesus had needed something, the disciples would have responded promptly. Jesus' answer stretched their compassionate imagination: "Whatever you did for one of the least of these brothers of mine, you did for me" (v. 40).

Compassion care covers a lot of "whatever."

CHAPTER 3

THE HOSPITABLE GRIEF SHARER

The opportunity to be present to people in grief is a privilege that [allows] one to be drawn into the richness of life. I, too, have been changed by the encounter.

—Alan Wolfelt, "Companioning Versus Treating," 15

A large church was recruiting volunteers for various ministries. Noticing a sign that read "Funeral ministry," I stopped at the table to ask what this church did for the grieving.

"Oh, we send a casserole. Then, a year later we send them a book on grief." The recruiter smiled and thrust a sign-up sheet at me. *Wow!* I thought as I walked away. *I hope it's a big casserole!*

Not only must we make room in our busy schedules, but we must also make room in our definition of hospitality. As Christine Pohl says in her book *Making Room: Recovering Hospitality as a Christian Tradition,* today we think of hospitality not as welcoming strangers, but as opening our homes to friends and family members. Seldom do we view it as a spiritual obligation or expression of Christianity.

Hospitality was so valued that it was a requirement for leadership in the Early Church (1 Tim. 3:2; Titus 1:8).

In the midst of the Nazi era in Germany, theologian Dietrich Bonhoeffer concluded that a hospitable person must be willing to face inconvenience. "We must be ready to allow ourselves to be interrupted by God," he said. "God will be constantly crossing our paths and canceling our plans by sending us people with claims and petitions" (*Life Together,* 99).

In the ancient world, without Holiday Inns and fast-food chains, travelers depended upon hospitality. In today's world, hospitality is essential to emotional and spiritual survival. Robert Benson described one group of Christians' response following the death of an infant: "As the news spread around town, people began to do the only thing they could: they began to pray. Many of them did so with their hands."

How can we "pray" with our hands?

"One came and sat with Mary Lou while she held Keenan and said good-bye to the sweet boy she had never really had a chance to say hello to. Another came to be on the telephone in the waiting room and make the calls that spread the word. . . . Someone else came to stay with the older children until Gary could get home with the terrible news instead of a new baby." Benson concludes, "Together, they 'prayed' the prayer of intercession, the prayer of shouldering the burdens of others" (*Living Prayer*, 135-36).

It may be hard for you to count such "deeds of love and kindness" as prayer unless you have survived your own Grief 101. But through such prayerful kindnesses, we discover we are part of a heavenly kingdom.

Perhaps you remember the words to that wonderful song by Ira B. Wilson: "Make me a blessing; make me a blessing. / Out of my life may Jesus shine."

Dare we sing, "Out of my caring acts may Jesus shine."

Dare we say yes? Dare we live out the songwriter's words, "Make me a blessing, O Savior, I pray. / Make me a blessing to someone *today*" (emphasis added). Through my acts of kindness—may Jesus show up!

I come to you
at the initiation of the Holy Spirit,
who through my eyes
through my ears
through my heart
through my hand,
and occasionally,
through my mouth,
would bring you comfort
and remind you
of the abiding presence of God
in this wilderness of grief.

Recently I read an essay on community by Kenneth Chaffin. In four decades of pastoring, he processed lots of grumbling about Sunday school classes. After retiring, Dr. Chaffin joined his wife in a Sunday school class and gained a new appreciation for Sunday school. He commented,

> So much more is going on than imparting biblical facts. The strength of the class was not in the quality of the Bible study, but in the community

that had been created and their ongoing care of each other. They helped each other deal with all the ups and downs of life. . . . Their love and concern for each other was real, and it was *concretized* with the giving of their time and energy to be supportive in a host of ways. And I saw this same thing happening in classes of all different age groups. What I observed could be done by any group that has learned to love each other ("From the Front Porch," 7).

These days, grievers look to a Sunday school class or small group because family members—supposedly the first line of support—are dealing with their own grief and may be emotionally, even physically, unavailable.

Yet, the testimony of many down through the ages, and more recently, is, "I don't know how we would have made it through this without the folks from the church."

Dr. Fred Craddock tells a story about arriving at a rural church for a weekend revival meeting just as a funeral was ending. The pastor introduced Craddock to the widow.

Craddock said, "This is no time for you to be meeting strangers. I'm sorry, and I'm really sorry about your loss. I know this will be a difficult time for you."

"It is. So I won't be at the services tonight, but I'll be there tomorrow night, and I'll be there on Sunday morning."

Craddock replied, "Oh, you don't need to."

"Yes, I do," the widow responded.

Craddock tried to clarify his words. "Well, what I meant to say was, I know it's a very hard time."

"I know it's hard. It's already hard, but you see, this is my church, and they're going to see that my children and I are okay."

Could a new widow confidently say of your congregation: "This is my church and they're going to see that my children and I are okay"?

Many grievers find great paradox between the choruses we sing, like "The Family of God," and the lived-out realities in contemporary fast-paced life. You, too, can concretize your membership in the family of God by sharing grief.

WISE WORDS FOR LOANING
"In a society which is much more inclined to help you hide your pain rather than to grow through it, it is necessary to make a very conscious effort to mourn.

—Henri Nouwen

CHAPTER 4

PADDING THE ROPES FOR GRIEVERS

God be in my head
and in my understanding.
God be in mine eyes
and in my looking.
God be in my mouth
and in my speaking.
God be in my heart
and in my thinking.
God be at mine end
and at my departing.

—From a Book of Hours (1514) in Doubleday, 460

People want to be helpful in the early days of loss. One of the first things they say to the bereaving is "Let me know if there's anything I can do."

One Old Testament example of courageous compassion care offers insight into servant hospitality.

In 587 BC Jeremiah the prophet landed in a cistern as punishment for predicting Jerusalem's capture by the Babylonians. Such a punishment was life-threatening. But Ebed-Melech, a Cushite eunuch, intervened.

My mother repeatedly counseled us, "Don't go sticking your nose in other people's business!" Apparently, Ebed-Melech's mother had not drilled that adage into him. Ebed-Melech approached King Zedekiah and bravely declared, "These men have acted wickedly in all they have done to Jeremiah the prophet" (Jer. 38:9). Ebed-Melech was persuasive. With the king's authorization, he recruited 30 men (38:10) to lift Jeremiah from the cistern.

Rather than dashing to the cistern, Ebed-Melech detoured to the royal rag room to secure old rags and worn-out clothes. When he arrived at the cistern, he cropped the life-saving rope to Jeremiah but also cascaded him with rags, telling him, "Put these old rags and worn-out clothes under your arms to pad the ropes" (v. 12).

What an example of creative sensitivity! Jeremiah had been lowered into the cistern by ropes. Those ropes had possibly bruised or broken his skin, particularly under his arms. Yanking Jeremiah out of this cistern could cause more rope burns and injury, possibly serious infection. Ebed-Melech not only was concerned about getting Jeremiah out of the well but also wanted to do so without further injuring the prophet.

An important goal in grief sharing is not simply to extract people from cisterns of grief as quickly as possible, especially since grief ministry is time-consuming and inconvenient. It's to "pad the ropes" so the reaved are not further injured.

HOW CAN A HELPER "PAD THE ROPES"?

Helpers must realize that the need for compassionate care lasts long after the initial 72 hours of traditional care. In fact, some bereaving will need long-term care. Some grievers are too numb initially to realize, let alone verbalize, needs; some are too independent to ask for help.

A song I often heard sung in my childhood, "Rescue the Perishing," identifies the need:

Down in the human heart,
Crushed by the tempter,
Feelings lie buried that grace can restore.
Touched by a loving heart,

Wakened by kindness,
Chords that are broken will vibrate once more.

—Fanny J. Crosby

It may be difficult for you to categorize grievers as "the perishing" who need rescuing. Helpers do not "rescue" bereaving from the necessary grief work that reconciles them with the loss. Helpers can, however, *accompany* them. They can make a difference by offering compassion care that touches grieving hearts and nurtures the seeds of hope for a better day.

Paul's words to the Corinthian Christians are often read at funerals: "Praise be to the God and Father of our Lord Jesus Christ, the Father of compassion and the God of all comfort, who comforts us in all our troubles" (2 Cor. 1:3-4). What a promise! However, Paul continued, *"so that* we can comfort those in any trouble with the comfort we ourselves have received from God" (v. 4, emphasis added). God comforts us . . . *so that.* So that what? So that we may share that same comfort with others. So that we may keep that compassion "in circulation." Paul's *so that* empowers us to offer compassion care in Jesus' name. The ancient observation of Christians, "Behold, how they love one another" today needs to cause non-Christians to conclude, "Behold, how they *care* for one another *in times of grief.*"

An old song by Frank E. Graeff titled "Does Jesus Care?" asks, "Does Jesus care when my heart is pained / Too deeply for mirth and song . . . ?" To every question the chorus exuberantly answers, "O yes, He cares; I know He cares! His heart is touched with my grief." And I believe his heart is touched by our care for those whose grief he notices.

Do you care enough to be inconvenienced? Do you care enough to experience another's grief up close? Do you care enough to learn the deficiency of the easy answers we spout as clichés? The God who invited Ebed-Melech to be part of a solution to Jeremiah's dilemma invites you to be part of a griever's solution. The bereaving are experiencing the emotional and spiritual equivalents of a cistern. They cannot get out on their own. The walls are too steep and slimy. They need *you* to be what Penelope Wilcock calls "a mediator of God's gentleness" (*Spiritual Care of Dying and Bereaved People*, 53).

"Don't wait to care. Being a follower of Jesus is about loving other people even when you doubt that your loving or your caring or your time or your gifts make any difference at all. Do you remember the story of the Good Samaritan? If he had waited until he had no doubts about the situation, that man would still be in the ditch" (Ronald M. Patterson, "The Positive Power of Doubt," 13).

WISE WORDS FOR LOANING

"Everyone must be given the opportunity to hurt out loud"

—Lady Bird Johnson, (Jan Jarboe Russell, *Lady Bird: A Biography of Mrs. Johnson*, 53).

PART 2

RESPONDING
WITH YOUR
HEART

WISE WORDS FOR LOANING
There are two important questions:
"Where do you hurt?"
and "How can I help?"

—Edwin S. Shneidman, MD

CHAPTER 5

BE THERE

I am only one,
But still I am one.
I cannot do everything,
But still I can do something;
And because I cannot do everything
I will not refuse to do the something that I can do.

—Edward Everett Hale,
cited in Bartlett, *Familiar Quotations*, 590

In your grieving process, you will gradually learn the people
you can count on for support and who are the ones who are
unwilling or incapable of providing assistance that is of any
benefit to you. Bereaved parents frequently speak of this,
often indicating surprise at who they thought were their
friends versus those who actually turned out to be.

—Theresa Huntley, *When Your Child Dies*, 40

As we have opportunity, let us do good to all people,
especially to those who belong to the family of believers.

—Gal. 6:10

You can make a difference in the life and grief of the bereaving. You can be there, not with words and explanations, but with presence. You can make a difference by walking in when others walk out. You can make a difference by walking at the griever's pace rather than yours.

Often people discount their ability to say or do the right thing. You cannot "fix" any grief. Grief will have to be lived out. No one permanently postpones grief. You cannot take away this grief from the bereaving.

Some people are good with words in difficult times of life. But the bereaving may not even hear their eloquent words or prayers. On the other hand, sometimes people who fumble for words say something that will sink deeply into the soul.

What you offer may be as welcomed as a life raft to a drowning person. Coming from you, it may be more acceptable than from a well-meaning stranger or a well-trained professional.

Paul, who knew a lot about grief, warned, "If I speak in the tongues of men and of angels, but have not love, I am only a resounding gong or a clanging cymbal" (1 Cor. 13:1). That could be rephrased, "If I encourage by using the words of well-known grief experts, but have not love, I am useless."

Some people cannot express their grief "nicely." Their words sting; their laments contain blunt language and exclamation marks. Some sling anger-drenched words in every direction—including toward those who are "only trying to help." Helpers must have thick skins *and* soft hearts. Sometimes helpers get caught in the crossfire and are wounded by the words. Some helpers who have been around the block diffuse the words, but others harbor them and replay them in show motion, reliving what they perceive as an "attack."

Richard Rohr is clear: the task of believers and helpers is to "receive the narrative." Admittedly, some will test your willingness to listen.

All grievers need safe places to work through their grief. For some it will be in a coffee shop, for others in a cemetery, over a shared sandwich and fruit, while walking or jogging, or while playing rigorous game of racquetball.

WHAT YOU CAN DO

- You can clear your schedule. You can make time for the grieving. While Paul says, "as we have opportunity," I think he would not disapprove of, "as we *make* opportunity."
- You can recognize that the words "I'm fine, thank you for asking" may be an invitation for you to stop and listen.

- You can invite God to be with you. I've often wondered what would happen if people, before walking into a funeral home for a visitation, paused and breathed a prayer: *May the words of my mouth . . .* It's possible to unload well-intentioned words and walk away feeling rather spiritually proud, unaware that the words will reverberate hurtfully in that griever's heart for hours, days, weeks, months to come.

- You can say, "I don't know what you're going through . . . but I'm willing to listen to anything you have to say." More than once when challenged by a griever, I have replied, "No, I don't know, but I'll never have any idea if you don't share your experience with me."

GRIEF SHARERS OFFER THEMSELVES

You didn't show up with prepackaged words;
you merely said, "I'm here."
You didn't say, "Call me if I can help";
you asked, "How can I help you?"
You didn't say, "God must know best";
you said, "God's got some explaining to do on this
*   one."*
You didn't quote scriptures;
you held my hand and got me a fresh cup of coffee.
You didn't walk away when I was angry;

you took the brunt of my words and my anger.
You didn't make everything "all better";
you made a difference.
You didn't give me any books or tracks or pamphlets;
you gave me big chunks of time.
You didn't try to answer my questions;
you admitted that you had your own.
You didn't offer platitudes and certaintudes;
you cleaned my bathroom.
You didn't hum any little feel-good choruses;
you sang, "Jesus loves you, this I know . . ."
on my answering machine.
You didn't try to be Holy Joe;
you were you, God's representative in this mess.
You didn't try to rush me through my grief;
you said, "In time. In time."
You didn't recite Kubler-Ross's stages of grief;
you made me look at my thumbprint
and said, "Your grief is just as unique."
You didn't say when I called, "Do you know what
time it is?";
you said, "What's on your mind?"
You never once reminded me that my grief inconvenienced you;
you kept assuring me, "I'm here for you."
You didn't quote scripture to me;

you lived out scripture to me.
I never had to ask, "Does Jesus care?"
because I knew Jesus cared through you.

Harold Ivan Smith

....

Blessed are the helpers who
are uniquely themselves.

CHAPTER 6

OFFER GIFTED WORDS

Spiritual carers have to learn the skill not only of being good communicators but also of enabling others to communicate.

—Penelope Wilcock
Spiritual Care of Dying and Bereaved People, 52

If fear of public speaking is first among Americans, fear of speaking to a griever is a close second. I'll tell you a secret: sometimes I don't know what to say even though I am a grief educator. There are no experts on grief when it comes to composing words.

Sometimes it is hard to beat silence. At least you never have to go back and apologize for inappropriate words.

The writer of Prov. 25 noted that the wise helper searches for the right word: "A word aptly spoken is like apples of gold in settings of silver" (v. 11), while the wrong word scrapes the raw linings of the soul. I wonder if he learned that insight after walking the grief path.

Sometimes we need to borrow words. It's hard to improve on what I call "gifted words" from people, such as the quotations scattered throughout this book.

What was helpful with one griever may not be as helpful with another. Sometimes what started out as a pile of words becomes a succinct, memorable gift.

Grief will be a watershed for friends and loved ones you know. It will leave permanent marks on personalities too. Your fear of saying the wrong thing may keep you from saying anything. You don't have to be eloquent. You need only be real and transparent. As James Miller notes, "Always the purpose of your talk is to invite *their* talk" (*The Art of Being a Healing Presence,* 40).

AVOID CLICHÉS AND PLATITUDES

Sensitive people would certainly not use profanity in front of grievers. But clichés and platitudes can be just as offensive. In some cases, they cause the griever to miss potentially helpful words that follow. Too many helpers use them as conversation jump starters. Clichés and platitudes are a type of shorthand that keep grievers and helpers from grappling with realities that can't always be corralled in words, sentences, and paragraphs.

Clichés fit into four general categories.

The generic. These are offered regardless of the circumstances of the death. "It was all for the best." "It's not for us to ask 'Why?'" "You're young—you can have more children." "Time heals all wounds." "I know just how you feel."

The spiritual. These are appeals to faith rootings. "It was God's will." "She's a flower in God's bouquet." "God never puts more on us than we can handle."

The admonitions. These are helpful hints. "Be strong." "Keep busy." "Think of all you have to be thankful for."

The laudatory. These focus on praising the griever's coping skills. "You're holding up so well." "You're so strong." "I couldn't handle this if I were in your shoes."

Helen Wilson Harris offers alternatives to clichés: "I'm sorry." "I'm thinking of you." "I know this is terribly hard—it must hurt so much." "I won't forget him [her]." "He [she] was very special because . . ." ("Congregational Care for the Chronically Ill, Dying and Bereaved," 41).

Many people are walking cliché-dispensers. They can discharge a barrage of clichés with startling speed. Sometimes helpers must bite their tongues in the presence of a cliché-spouter. This is no time to "correct" anyone, but it may be time to change the environment creatively.

A TIME TO BE SILENT

Sometimes ministering to others simply means being quiet.

How comfortable are you with silence? Do you think you always have to say something? Will your "something" change any essential facts or circumstances? Too many grievers have experienced a beautiful silence shattered by an inane cliché or observation. Grief sharers must be able to tolerate silence.

Many grievers need the gift of silence. Many more grievers need the gift of a shared silence.

Sitting alone together in a shared silence can be healing for both griever and helper. This is why Jews "sit Shivah." Friends go "to the house of mourning"— the primarily residence of the chief mourner—but are not expected to speak, except perhaps to offer an "I'm so sorry." They are, however, expected to "sit awhile."

In a world with so much clutter and noise, you make a difference by sharing silence.

....

*Blessed are the helpers who weigh words carefully
and avoid clichés and platitudes.*

....

"Sit down.
Hush up!
Stop trying to fix things!
Be still for a while."
—Lois Wagner, RN

CHAPTER 7

Grant Permission

*We are doing a good job with grief when we are crying our
eyes out and making the whole world nervous in the process.
Grief is not an enemy to be avoided—
it is a process that leads to healing.*

—Doug Manning, *The Funeral*, 16

There is no such thing as a bad question.
*The issue is not with the questions we ask, or even how we ask
them. The issue is where we go with questions. Any question
that brings us to God for an answer is a good question.*

Dave Dravecky, *When You Can't Come Back*, 144

*About the ninth hour Jesus cried out in a loud voice . . .
"My God, my God, why have you forsaken me?"*

—Matt. 27:46

The young boy had tried so hard to "Be strong." He did well until the time to leave the funeral chapel for the cemetery. Then he lost it. His grandfather had filled an important place in his life. Immediately he realized he was the only one of the male cousins crying. Noticing his distress, his Sunday school teacher slipped over and put her arm around his shoulder and walked beside him. With only two words, "It's okay," she gave him permission to grieve differently than his cousins.

I was that boy. I've never forgotten Hazel Belle-baum giving me that permission to grieve that snowy day after Christmas 1959. For Mrs. Bellebaum, it was merely the right thing to do as a caring adult. For me, it was an eloquent gift. You do not have to have a string of degrees behind your name or credentials on your office wall to give permission to grieve.

Grievers live a culture that not only watches things happen but also encourages someone to "comment" on what just happened. Immediately after the terrorist attacks on the Pentagon and the World Trade Center on September 11, 2001, the airways were filled with the professionals doing sound bytes; talk shows offered an opportunity for amateurs to give opinions. What happens after a national tragedy often happens in an individual's tragedy too. Many people feel free to "comment," not realizing it is borderline criticism.

"How do you think Joan is doing?" There are several variations on this basic question. Too commonly, the bereaving are forced to go underground with their grief. Subtly we say, "If you must grieve, at least do it in private—not where we can see it and definitely not where we can feel it." Grievers who thoroughly grieve make many of us nervous. We say things like "What? You're *still* grieving? Why, it's been weeks [months]!"

A "What?" can reverberate like thunder. Doug Manning captured this thought in his great book titled *Don't Take My Grief Away from Me.* Sometimes the grief sharer needs to say, "Don't let anyone [spouse, family member, religious leader, or me] take your grief from you!"

Manning points out, "You deserve it, and you must have it. If you had a broken leg, no one would criticize you for using crutches until it was healed. If you had major surgery, no one would pressure you to run a marathon the next week. Grief is a major wound. It does not heal overnight. You must have the time and the crutches until you heal" (65).

Ellen Goodman points out, "Whatever our natural passion for emotional efficiency, for quality-time parents and one-minute managers, there simply are no one-minute grievers" ("Mourning Gets the Bum's Rush," B7).

Grief sharers can give permission for grievers to take time to heal. It takes time to thoroughly grieve.

BE COMFORTABLE WITH QUESTIONS

If many Americans are anxious to stop a tear flow, they are really antsy about questions, especially those that include *God* or are asked in a demanding tone of voice.

A griever named Kimberly describes her first encounter with asking why: "You would have thought I had cussed or denied the Virgin Birth. My minister was all over me: 'Who are you to question God?' I was not questioning God. I was just wanting to know where God was when my six-year-old grandson ran into the path of the car. But Millie—God bless her—said one day over coffee, 'You know, I asked a million questions when my son died. I have never let up asking, "Why?" I intend to pester God with "Whys" until my dying breath.'"

Nothing is wrong with asking "Why?" Jesus himself affirmed this. Matthew 27:46 tells us that at the Crucifixion, "About the ninth hour Jesus cried out in a loud voice, 'My God, my God, why have you forsaken me?'"

Alan D. Wolfelt points out, "Some questions have answers. Some do not. Actually, the healing occurs in the opportunity to pose the questions, not necessarily in answering them. Helpers can give the bereaving permission to keep asking, and helpers can keep hearing out the questions. Again. And again" ("Understanding Grief: Helping Yourself Heal").

In many ways, becoming a griever is to be initiated into a fraternity: The Order of the Questioners—a group with no racial, ethnic, religious, age, or gender barriers.

LET THEM CRY

Five-year-old Elliot kept rattling the locked bedroom door. "Mom, what are you doing? I want to come in." Nancy, his mother, tried to explain that she needed some time alone. Finally, she unlocked the door, and her son came in to sit beside her. When she began to cry, he responded, "Mom, it's okay to be sad and cry when someone you really love dies."

"I couldn't believe it!" she told me. "My child gave me permission to grieve. How did he get so wise at five years of age?"

Many are uncomfortable with tears. Frances found this to be true. She explains, "People keep asking me why I go to the cemetery so much. My daughter says, "He's not there! So why go?' I go because it's the only public place I can cry without having to apologize."

We are socially conditioned to thrust a tissue with the first tear. That prompts most grievers to apologize for tears: "I'm sorry" or "Forgive me" or "Pardon me."

We're well trained, we Americans. It's tempting for the grief sharer to go along with the apology. Instead, apologies should be challenged: "There's nothing to be sorry for. Tears are natural."

As a helper, some of the most healing words you can offer are "There's nothing to apologize for." In fact, a Jewish proverb says, "What soap is for the body, tears are for the soul" (*Leo Rosten's Treasury of Jewish Quotations,* 449).

With some grievers, remind them that Jesus cried at His friend Lazarus's death (John 11:35). If Jesus cried, that gives any griever, female or male, permission to cry. Sometimes a griever knows this but needs to be reminded.

Too often, helpers stumble over their words because they're trying so hard not to say anything that would provoke tears. Tears are one way we punctuate our grief thoughts.

....

Blessed are the helpers who give grievers permission to feel pain and to cry and to ask questions.

CHAPTER 8

Receive Laments and Stories

Each lifetime is the pieces of a jigsaw puzzle. For some there are more pieces. For others, the puzzle is more difficult to assemble. But know this: you do not have within yourself all the pieces to your puzzle. Everyone carries with them at least one and probably many pieces to someone else's puzzle. . . . And when you present your piece, which is worthless to you, to another, whether you know it or not, whether they know it or not, you are a messenger from the Most High.

—Lawrence Kushner, *Living a Life That Matters*, 142-43

When will you end these speeches?
Be sensible, and then we can talk.

Bildad the Shuhite to Job, Job 18:2

Lorenzo Albacete, a staff member in a large church, answered the phone late in the night. The caller's sister had died in a plane crash. It didn't seem fair, she said, and she wasn't sure she believed in God. Nevertheless, she just wanted to talk with someone. Would Pastor Albacete come?

Pastor Albacete not only went but also stopped to pick up doughnuts and coffee. He recalls, "I wasn't there to discuss theology, to propose intellectual answers to the questioning in her heart. I told her that although I believed that her sister had not died forever, I shared the demands of her grief, and we sat in her kitchen to eat the doughnuts and drink the coffee" ("Good Grief and Bad," 22).

Victoria Alexander reminds helpers that every griever has three essential needs:

To find words to express the loss;

To say the words aloud;

To know that the words have been heard (*Words I Never Thought to Speak*, xx).

Many grievers have encountered a "language cop" citing them for improper speech. Job, having lost all 10 of his children, laments, "My days have passed, my plans are shattered, and so are the desires of my heart" (17:11). He concludes, "Where then is my hope? Who can see any hope for me?" (v. 15).

Bildad, who probably had never had training in communications, could not simply receive Job's words (18:2). He had to "correct" Job. Possibly, while Job was lamenting, Bildad was composing a challenge: "Whoa, Job. Let's get a couple of things straight."

Few of us are gifted in receiving laments. Most of us want to pretend any lament to be an adult equivalent of a child's booboo and "make it all better."

Sometimes helpers who are skilled listeners may have their image of the deceased shattered when a loved one tells "the other side." The common warning to "speak no ill of the dead" sometimes interferes with truth.

Sometimes there's nothing to say in response. The wise listener may ask for time to think about what has been disclosed, and the helper "takes it to the Lord in prayer." Corrie ten Boom often prayed, "Now, Father, you have heard what we have been talking about. You know the need. We thank you for listening. We thank you for caring. And we trust you to supply us" (Memorial service, April 22, 1983). That can be an excellent model for grief sharers.

This skill is demonstrated by Jesus' discourse with two bereaving disciples on the Emmaus Road following his resurrection. He asked, "What are you discussing together as you walk along?" (Luke 24:17). He gave them a chance to air their disappointments. They were obviously doubting the veracity of the resurrection reports they had heard.

Wanda's friend Gloria was a lifesaver when Wanda was going through grief. "Gloria was incredible," she said. "She simply let me rant and rave and ramble. I kept expecting her to say, 'That's it—I've had it with you!' But she didn't. The times when she didn't know what to say, she took my hand, squeezed it, or poured another cup of coffee. In 10 minutes with her I felt as though I unloaded on her. But she was there for me. She didn't give up on me."

Grievers not only need to air their laments, but also they sometimes just need to tell anecdotes about their loved ones. Again, to listeners these stories may not seem to have a point. But for the griever, speaking of the loved one is important. In *The Heart of Grief,* Thomas Attig explains, "As we remember what we love about those who have died, we welcome them back into our lives even thought we are apart. We begin to learn how to love them in new ways. In memory we can cherish them. We can carry them with us into the future" (27).

....

Blessed are the helpers who willingly receive the lament and the stories of the bereaving.

CHAPTER 9

APPLAUD BABY STEPS

One never notices what has been done;
one can only see what remains to be done.

—Marie Curie, *Treasury of Women's Quotations*, 13

And there, where they were living, I sat among them
for seven days—overwhelmed.

—Ezek. 3:15

The little boy had been told to clean his room. Or else. For the longest time he stood there. After a few moments his mother called from the kitchen, "Well?" The boy responded, "I don't know where to begin!"

So it is with many bereaving who feel overwhelmed with incredible expectations, responsibilities, and "to do" lists. In Arnold Lobel's delightful children's book, Toad is in the dumps because his house is a mess and he has so much work to do. He pulls the covers over his head and mumbles, "Tomorrow."

Frog suggests a gradual approach. Toad asks, "If I wash my dishes right now, then I will not have to wash them tomorrow, will I?" Frog goads him into further action until at the end of the story Toad exclaims, "Now I can save tomorrow for something that I really want to do" (*Days with Frog and Toad*, 14).

Grievers who serve as executors of the loved one's estate face an incredible bureaucracy of government and insurance paperwork. Many can be overwhelmed by the mountain of paperwork. Form after form must be complete, accurate, and appropriately filed and submitted. In fact, some individuals cannot do their grief work *and* the paperwork as well.

"Making headway" is an important assessment; for others, it's "making a dent." Sometimes it takes a helper to bring perspective to all the details, as Beverly found. She explained: "Margie came over and helped

me go through my husband's stuff. She folded and
boxed and never prodded me. There were some things
I ended up taking out of the boxes, deciding I wasn't
quite ready to let go of. Graciously, she unfolded and
put the items back on the hanger or in a drawer. She
knew when to let me be. After a long afternoon, I
think we got two boxes packed. She laughed and said,
'Well, that's two more boxes than when we started.'"

Blessed are the helpers whose hands are always
ready to applaud the baby steps of the bereaving.

WISE WORDS FOR LOANING

"I am convinced, more than ever, that our culture has labeled
as 'weird' some of the most wonderful, precious, and sensitive
acts of grief. Now I understand, it is imperative to give ourselves
permission to grieve in our own time and in our own way."

—Barbara Roberts

PART 3

RESPONDING
WITH YOUR
ACTIONS

Grief is complicated by "good intentions"
that never become loving acts of kindness.

CHAPTER 10

VOLUNTEER FOR IMMEDIATE INITIAL PRESENCE

Throwing caution to the wind, they [friends, Steve and Kathy] walked into the house and embraced me in tears, though they had no idea of what to say to comfort me and the children. They chose to make themselves available, vulnerable, and present to our suffering. They became a part of our brokenness.

—Gerald Sittser, *A Grief Disguised*, 155

Just having a normal human being in the general vicinity can mean a great deal.

—Linda Richman, *I'd Rather Laugh*, 46

Saul's son Jonathan went to David at Horesh and helped him find strength in God.

—1 Sam. 23:16

The notification of a death is like the fire bell summoning volunteer firemen in a rural community. In *Bowling Alone,* Robert D. Putnam argues that the demise of bowling leagues is a reflection of the growing individualism and isolation common in this country. Yet within moments of the 2001 terrorist attacks in New York City and Washington, D.C., millions of independent Americans were asking that timeless question, "What can I do?"

When a friend, neighbor, or loved one has died, one of the first gifts a helper can offer is to call the residence—or if you know the family well, go to the residence—to volunteer immediate practical help. From the beginning, grievers need to know they're not alone. In the first moments or hours, they may need help with simple tasks—to pick up a child from school, to answer the phone, and so on. Some grievers may be reluctant to accept assistance. Some will need time to understand the gravity of a loss. People who are proud of "looking out for number one" don't easily give up control.

A friendly face in the midst of chaos can be a calming blessing: "Oh, thank God—*you're* here." In some cases, several volunteers may already be on the scene; you may decide your help will be needed more down the road. So write your name and phone numbers on a piece of paper. Yes, the person has dialed it a thousand times. But in grief, numbers do not always register.

Following the April 1999 Columbine High School shootings in Littleton, Colorado, I was touched by the kind people who reached out to the shooters' families, who were in shock and grief as well. Because no one was answering the phone, two friends scribbled a sign and stuck it in the Klebolds' yard facing the house: "Tom and Sue, we love you. We're here for you. Call us."

WHAT TO DO?

"I don't know where to begin" is a common frustration many helpers share. Some may be immobilized by the complexity of a loss. A Japanese proverb says, "The longest journey begins with the first step." I would rephrase it, "The longest journey begins with the decision to admit that you don't know what to say or do." Then you can ask, "What is the first step in *this* situation?"

Grief sharers ask three questions: What can I do? What can I *not* do? and What shall I do *first?*

In some grief, the great need is for a "take charge" person to serve at least temporarily until a family member arrives. As a helper, you may not be able to do everything, but you can do something, such as answering the telephone and taking messages, answering the door, comforting a child, loading the dishwasher, running an errand, or tidying up around the griever's home.

Some people are good at offering initial help—when the primary griever may be in shock, unable to talk. Others are good at "down the road" help.

Helpful acts free the primary grievers to focus on active grieving. Blessed is the grieving family who gets a chief organizer, or the lead grief sharer, to orchestrate compassionate acts of care. This may be facilitated by asking, "How can I best help you *now?*"

Admittedly, many grievers will not know how to answer. In some cases, when the helper knows the bereaving well, it may be best to proceed without asking.

Ask questions, such as "Have you eaten? When did the children eat? When was the last time you had something to drink? (Many grievers get dehydrated.) Who needs to be notified?"

A griever named Tom remembers: "My friend Sara showed up asking, 'What can I do?' I have no idea how I answered. What I do know is that we never had to lift our hand for a thing. She took charge without 'taking over.' And she must have done something right—we've survived so far."

Blessed are the helpers who show up and anticipate what needs to be done.

send cards
and notes

Sympathy cards express your concern, but there is no substitute for your own personal words. . . . These words will be a loving gift to your grieving, words that will be reread and remembered for years.

—Alan D. Wolfelt, "Helping a Friend in Grief," 28

The Teacher searched to find just the right words.

—Eccles. 12:10

On Wednesday night, September 12, 2001, the day after the attacks on the World Trade Center in New York City and the Pentagon in Washington, D.C., and the crash of the hijacked airliner in Pennsylvania, children whose parents were attending a community prayer service were asked to make cards to send to the victims. One little girl worked intently. The teacher leading the experience was stunned by her card:

To: Mr. Osama Bin Laden. We love you and we forgive you. You need to turn your heart toward Jesus.

David Unruh calls sympathy cards a "strategic social action" ("Death and Personal History," 340), something we can do *now*. Millions of bereavement cards are sent every year. An unwritten commandment motivates many: "Get thee to a card shop!"

Good cards capture the little girl's components: (1) We love you. (2) We care. (3) Turn your heart toward Jesus.

Researchers have identified factors influencing the sending of a sympathy card:

- More young adults are sending cards than before.
- More people want to receive cards than before.
- Peaceful nature scenes are most popular.
- Older adults are more likely to add a handwritten note.

- The words *dead, died,* and *killed* are absent on sympathy cards.
- Senders want to reassure the bereaved that he or she "has the sender's deepest, heartfelt, sincere, understanding sympathy for the loss."
- Senders hope this particular card and the thoughts behind it will bring comfort ("The Sympathy Card as Cultural Assessment of American Attitude Toward Death, Bereavement and Extending Sympathy: A Replicated Study," 121-32).

Bereavement cards are sent in three waves:

Early cards. Some grief sharers keep cards on hand. For other helpers, picking the right card to send is an important task. In fact, some skim card after card looking for one that's "just right." I suspect searching for the right card is therapeutic for some helpers.

Milled grief cards. Many helpers promptly send cards immediately after the notification of the death. However, many of those cards are not read or even remembered. Later, after the shock has worn a bit, many grievers turn their attention to reading the cards.

Ann Landers suggests that grievers "take" the card to the bereaving rather than mail it. This way, a card will "jump start" a conversation, because the grieving need someone to talk to and share with.

Down-the-road cards. Bea Decker wrote *After the Flowers Are Gone.* Many grievers could write a book titled *After the Cards Have Stopped Coming.* Part of the American zeal to "be over" grief is encouraging people to "not get mired down" in grief or "time to move on." So "Thinking of you today" cards, especially on those difficult first special days, holidays, and anniversaries, will be appreciated.

Certainly cards should be personalized, but scribbled clichés can wound as much as verbalized ones. Helpers may want to borrow an encouraging Moroccan expression, "May God give you the patience to endure the pain" or a Georgian-Russian condolence, "Your sorrow is close to our hearts." I often write, "May God give you strength sufficient to meet the demands of *this* day.

I came across two binders, one containing some of the letters and cards we received after my son passed away. . . . I cannot remember all of the sentiments that were expressed verbally and who exactly came to express them. However, these letters are a timeless record of those who wrote and the beautiful sentiments they expressed.

—Aaron Levine, *To Comfort the Bereaved*, 81

....

Blessed are the helpers who send cards and notes— and keep on sending them.

CHAPTER 12

Remember in a Tangible Way

Say it with flowers.
A contribution to any worthwhile charity is
a fitting memorial to the memory of the deceased.

—Earl A. Grollman, *Concerning Death,* 128

May the Lord show mercy to the household
of Onesiphorus, because he often refreshed me.

—2 Tim. 1:16

Flowers have long been a *social* expression of condolence. Before embalming became common, flowers had a practical function: to mask odors associated with decomposition. While the Greeks and Romans carried funeral cypress palms in funeral processions, early Christians chose palm and olive branches as a reminder of Jesus' entry into Jerusalem and his victory over death.

Romans placed a wreath of flowers on the head as an honor. The early Christians placed flowers over the body, probably to cover up bodily discharges.

Sending flowers gives a grief sharer something practical to do. Before the commercial floral industry developed, friends made bouquets from their own gardens or planted flowers on the grave.

Alan Wolfelt considers flowers another "ousted symbol" like the armband or wreath on the door or women wearing black for a year. "Today we opt for the more practical but less spiritual monetary donation" (*Creating Meaningful Funeral Ceremonies*, 9).

Still, for many, flowers communicate caring when a friend cannot find words. Moreover, sending flowers is a documentable act of hospitality. By sending flowers, the family immediately knows of your condolence; with donations to charities, it could be weeks or months before notification.

Flowers stimulate conversation. Flowers are conversation jump starters at funeral rituals. An observation such as "All these beautiful flowers! Mary would
have loved them" may be enough to elicit a "You're
right about that. How did you know Mary?" Com-
menting on flowers allows safe, unobtrusive inter-
action with the family, with friends, and even with
strangers.

Given the growing acceptance of direct disposal,
graveside services, or private services, some helpers
send flowers or potted plants—to the residence. Some
sensitive helpers send flowers on the anniversary of a
death or on other special days. Flower sending is important to those who cannot attend a visitation or ritual.

DONATE TO A DESIGNATED CHARITY

Donating to a designated charity also gives friends
a positive way to show comfort and support to the bereaved family long after the rituals. Memorial gifts
reconfirm community programs valued by the deceased (Gerald L. Euster, "Memorial Contributions:
Remembering the Elderly Deceased and Supporting the Bereaved," 169-79). Some grief sharers think
memorial gifts are a more lasting expression of grief.
One lady recalls, "I haven't forgotten, months later,
the notices coming from so many charities in honor of

my husband. Just little reminders of how much he was loved and missed."

Helpers can donate at any time. Some find that giving to a memorial on anniversaries, birthdays, or special days is a "living remembrance" (Euster, "Memorial Contributions," 175). Donations offer a means to express condolences for helpers who belatedly learn of the death. Although a family may designate a specific charity, that does not limit helpers from giving in the deceased's name to other charities.

In some circumstances, grief sharers donate toward funeral expenses or to an educational fund for the children of the deceased.

Blessed are the helpers who show love tangibly by sending flowers or donating to designated charities.

WISE WORDS FOR LOANING
"Death is not a period that ends the great sentences of life,
but a comma that punctuates it to more lofty significance.
God is able . . . to transform dark and desolate valleys
into sunlit paths of inner peace."
—Martin Luther King, Jr.

CHAPTER 13

ATTEND THE RITUALS

When Larry's colleague told this story, she led the gathered congregation in remembering their husband, father, son, and friend. He was remembered—put back together—through her words, through the words of others who knew him . . . and through music and mutual embraces. On a certain afternoon in a certain year, a certain community, gathered just this once for just this purpose, remembered one particular man. . . . He took his place among them again, now not as flesh but as memory.

—Dorothy Bass, *Receiving the Day,* 115-16

Once a friend was expected to attend the trio of rituals: visitation, funeral, *and* committal. These days, ritual attendance is generally multiple choice—one of the above, not all three. In rural communities, ethnic communities, and small-town America there may be greater expectations for attendance.

Go for the deceased's family. If attending was "paying your respects," not attending was seen as disrespect to the deceased and to the family. One study on American attitudes about funeral rituals discloses a significant decline in individuals attending funerals (Susan Daniels, "Wirthlin Study Tracks Consumer Attitude Trends," 7). For many friends, the funeral or memorial service is *the* most important ritual.

Go for others. Others will let nothing prevent them from attending, because the bereaved need others. For the memorial of Peter Alderman, a Bloomsbury employee who died in the World Trade Center attacks, because airlines were not flying, two friends drove from San Francisco to Armonk, New York, in two-and-a-half days to be present for their friend's gathering. That's an amazing gift of presence these days, when some will not drive across town to attend.

Go for yourself. Some friends conclude that attendance at a ritual is "the least I can do" as a friend. If you can't attend, make some time for "individual mourning practices" (Jo-Anne Grabowski and Thomas T. Frantz, "Latinos and Anglos: Cultural Experiences of Grief Intensity," 282). You could pause at the time of the services and reflect.

Henry T. Close said of one funeral he attended, "I was there to affirm the life and death of my friend; to acknowledge the suffering that infused his whole being, and his ultimate protest against the world and its emptiness; to say to his family, 'In my limited way, I stand with you in your bewildered suffering'" ("A Funeral Service," 82-83).

....

Blessed are the helpers who attend the rituals.

WISE WORDS FOR LOANING

"Consciously remembering those who have died is the key that opens our hearts, that allows us to love them in new ways. . . . as we remember what we love about those who have died, we welcome them back into our lives even though we are apart."

—Thomas Attig. (2000). *The heart of grief: Death and the search for lasting love.* New York: Oxford University Press, 27.

CHAPTER 14

Pray

A place is reserved in Heaven for those
who weep but cannot pray.

—Jewish proverb
Leo Rosten's Treasury of Jewish Quotations, 364

There are prayers that help us last through the day or endure
the night. There are prayers of friends and strangers that give
us strength for the journey, and there are prayers that
yield our will to a will greater than our own.

—George W. Bush at the Washington National Cathedral
"Bush's Speech," A12

Pray continually.

—1 Thess. 5:17

"I cannot pray anymore" grieving people often confess. Sometimes, like a drowning swimmer, they have to relax and let others pray for them. In grief, few are experts at praying. We are all beginners and bunglers, groping in our emotional darkness for words.

Joyce Rupp is so honest: "At the time when we most need to experience the tender compassion and strengthening comfort of our God, we very often feel a great distance in this relationship" (*The Cup of Our Life: A Guide for Spiritual Growth*, 98).

We know about the encouragement to "ask, knock, seek" in Scripture. Jerry Porter, whose daughter Amy died 20 days before her wedding, adds "plead and even badger" to the list. "We must ask the hurting person what he or she wants the Lord to do, and then pray a simple, mustard-seed-faith prayer" ("Commission: Saints Suffer Too," 49).

So what can a helper do?

A helper prays *for* the grieving. This must be more than a mumbled "I will pray for you" at a visitation. Try putting a small sticker on your telephone so that every time you make a call you'll be reminded.

A helper prays *with* the grieving. I've never forgotten Mrs. Schoenlaub at my father's visitation. After offering her condolences to my mother, she asked, "Mary, what can I do for you?"

My mother replied, "Just pray for me."

Mrs. Schoenlaub said, "Would it be all right if we prayed right now, right here?" Five feet from my father's casket, Mrs. Schoenlaub prayed a prayer that I suspect caused God to say, "Shhh—I want to hear this." Few people heard her pray that night in the parlor at Ratterman's, but God did. And my mother did.

Many people promised "to pray"—Mrs. Schoenlaub *prayed*.

....

Blessed are the helpers who pray.

PRAYERS FOR LOANING
"God, where are you in *this?*"
—Joan Chittister

"God, stay close."
—David Wolpe

CHAPTER 15

PROVIDE FOOD: A BASIC OF LIFE

Nothin' says lovin' like somethin' from the oven!

—Pillsbury commercial

*"I was hungry and you gave me something to eat,
I was thirsty and you gave me something to drink." . . .
The righteous will answer him, "Lord, when did we see you
hungry and feed you?" . . . The King will reply,
"I tell you the truth, whatever you did for one of the
least of these brothers of mine, you did for me."*

—Matt. 25:35, 37, 40

When my mother died, I was not hungry. But the meal provided by the ladies of my mother's church gave our family a chance to gather around the tables and eat and, more importantly, to talk. Although I had been away from that congregation for 30 years, I recognized by taste the food from the church potlucks of my boyhood—good food made by loving hands and caring hearts. It made that tough day just a little bit easier. It would not have been nearly the same if we had gone to a restaurant.

A unique connection exists between food and comfort; we all have our own "works for me" comfort foods. It's especially comforting when the food is homemade. Homemade says, "You went to all the trouble."

Unfortunately, we live in an era when everyone is incredibly busy. So instead of heading to the kitchen—as my mother's generation did—helpers drop by the deli or the drive-through to pick up a bucket of this or tray of that.

Many helpers remember not only preparing the food, but also reaching for the masking tape to write a name on the bottom so that the dish, pan, or tray can be returned to the owner. Now we rely on plastic, tin, paper, or other disposable containers, thinking they save the time involved in washing real dishes, bowls, and plates.

Actually, the washing and returning had a secondary ritual. That action gave the bereaving a chance to say to the donor, "Thank you for preparing this" and opened the door to further dialogue. If the helper replied, "You're welcome. Do you have time for a cup of coffee?" the returning exchange gave many helpers a chance to ask, "How are you doing?"

Cooking and baking gives people a sense of "This may not be much, but it's something I *can* do." Food is so basic as a delivery mechanism. The old admonition "Eat something—you'll feel better" becomes "Make something—you'll feel better."

HELP THE GRIEVER EAT

"Who feels like eating at a time like this?" the griever moans in the hours and days following a death. Sometimes a caring individual has to monitor the griever's food intake. Only a close friend can insist, "You need to eat *something*."

Helpers also pay attention to eating habits long after the rituals. Many bereaving, rather than facing the reminder of the loss by eating alone, nibble on junk foods or fast foods. Some do not feel like cooking, even for children. Some grievers forget to eat. While some lose weight, others eat everything in sight to numb the pain.

Meals at church. In churches with traditions of fellowship meals and potlucks, grievers find it difficult to participate. "Too many memories" one woman explained. Sensitive grief sharers say, "Why don't you go *with us*? I've made plenty." Even though an individual has been to a hundred potlucks in a church, to a griever a potluck now takes on a different feel.

Grief sharers are aware that the opportunity for misunderstandings over hospitality are enormous. Newcomers to an area and/or to your church may have come from churches or communities that provide many meals to the grieving.

Long-aft-the-rituals meals. Caring friends express hospitality by inviting grievers to meals weeks and months afterward. Sensitive helpers may suggest a new restaurant rather than a memory-soaked favorite. In selecting a restaurant, friends pay attention to atmosphere. Noisy, crowded restaurants are seldom conducive to talking or venting emotions. Long waits in crowded waiting areas may further stress the griever.

Holidays. Grief sharers monitor holiday eating plans. Some bereaving might welcome a chance to eat with you or your family; others, however, find your happiness only reminds them of what they once had. Invite them—even if they say no.

....

Blessed are helpers who make sure grievers eat and who eat with grievers.

CHAPTER 16

EDUCATE YOURSELF ABOUT GRIEF

*I no longer assume that people experience a universal
sequence of stages or tasks following loss or that the process
of grieving can usefully be viewed as eventuating
in an end state of "recovery."*

—Robert Neimeyer, *Lessons of Loss*, 84

Then Abraham rose up from beside his dead wife.

—Gen. 23:33

Some people think that when Moses came down from Mount Sinai, he brought not only the Ten Commandments but also the five stages of grief. Denial, anger, bargaining, acceptance, and growth have been widely interpreted as *the* stages through which every griever must pass.

This is a significant misinterpretation of this work by Elizabeth Kubler-Ross. Increasingly, attention is being given to the concept of "tasks" of grief, developed by J. William Worden. The tasks are more active than stages and suggest possibilities and options to grievers.

To accept the reality of the loss. Sooner or later, grievers must "own" the reality that a loved one has died. Not only must they intellectually acknowledge the loss, but they must emotionally acknowledge it too (Theresa Huntley, *When Your Child Dies*, 19).

To work through to the pain of grief. The bereaving must go to the depths of the pain rather than avoid it. Pain deferred is pain intensified.

To adjust to an environment in which the person is missing. And continues to be missing.

To emotionally relocate and move on with life. "Move on" does not mean "get over." Abraham's action illustrates this task. When Sarah died at 127 years of age, "Abraham went to mourn for Sarah and to weep over her" (Gen. 23:3). We then read, "Then

Abraham *rose up* from beside his dead wife" (v. 4, emphasis added).

For those who have the hope of heaven, the death of a loved one whose life was a witness to God's grace, relocation is much easier: To be absent from the body, the apostle Paul insisted, is to be present with the Lord (see 2 Cor. 5:8). However, some do not have such an assurance; for them, relocation includes the possibility of hell. One gift of a grief sharer is to commend the deceased to God's grace. That is why the burial is called "the committal."

Blessed are helpers who familiarize themselves with what it means to grieve.

WISE WORDS FOR LOANING
"You close on a house. You don't close on a death."
—Peggy Broxterman

CHAPTER 17

Know Resources
for Referral

Mourning is not an illness,
is not a weakness
is not a self indulgence
or reprehensible bad habit,
but rather mourning is
an essential psychological process
that must be recognized
and facilitated.

—Patrick J. Farmer, "Bereavement Counseling," 32

Just as God chooses to heal us through a skilled physician,
so He chooses to heal us through a skilled psychologist.

—Paul G. Cunningham, Sermon,
Mother's Day, 1979, Olathe, Kansas

In a culture that prizes individualism, it is difficult to realize we cannot complete the grief process alone. We need a companion who is well acquainted with the trail.

I've noticed on cruises that as we come into a particular port, the captain turns control of the ship over to a harbor "pilot," an expert on *that* harbor. One of the greatest gifts you can give the bereaving is the name of a good counselor. You may want to check out costs, insurance copayment options, or human services referrals in the workplace. Not every counselor or psychologist can effectively help the bereaving.

Offer to accompany a griever on the first visit to a counselor. Take something to read in the waiting room. Pray for the griever as you wait. Remind him or her that going to a counselor is as natural as going to an ophthalmologist for sight problems, an audiologist for hearing problems, or a dermatologist for skin problems.

If grievers need to be able to find the words for the loss and say the words aloud, one of the safest places for many grievers is in a grief support group or mutual help grief group. A grief group can be like an oasis to a weary traveler in the desert because some group member has walked that portion of the grief path. The paradox is that the new griever, in time, will offer support and care to others in the group.

Admittedly, some have had poor previous experiences in groups. So as a helper, you may have to hear the concerns and urge the griever, "Give this group a chance."

KNOW GOOD BOOKS TO RECOMMEND

A good book is a welcome companion for grievers and for helpers. Good books offer insights into a grief experience. For example, I learned much about widowhood by reading Joan Rivers' *Bouncing Back*. A good book on grief can be like a life preserver. You may want to skim one so you can mark passages you think may be meaningful.

A book is an act of kindness that keeps giving. For helpers who have taken their laps around the grief track, it may increase the likelihood of a book being read if a note from the giver is included, such as "This helped me when _____ died."

Do not put a time limit on a book being read. We read like we grieve—*at our own pace.* Some take their time in getting to a new book, preferring to stay with a tested favorite the way a child clings to a comforting blanket. Donate a copy of the book to a church or public library. Some grievers in tight financial transitioning need to borrow books. Your gift hopefully will have a short "shelf" life. A book donated to a library is a great way to memorialize a friend or loved one.

....

Blessed are the helpers who can confidently recommend
skilled counselors and support groups and books.

WISE WORDS FOR LOANING

"If we are still breathing, it is too early to tell the
ultimate impact of any event in our lives."

—John R. Claypool

CHAPTER 18

GO TO THE GRAVE OR SCATTERING AREA

You should see it till the very end. Avoid the temptation of a tidy leavetaking in a room, a cemetery chapel, at the foot of the altar. None of that. Don't dodge it because of the weather. We've fished and watched football in worse conditions. It won't take long. Go to the hole in the ground. Stand over it. Look into it. Wonder. And be cold. But stay until it's over. Until it is done.

—Thomas Lynch, "A Serious Undertaking," 197

On the first day of the week, very early in the morning, the women took the spices they had prepared and went to the tomb.

—Luke 24:1

The Church has long appreciated the burial places of believers. Early Christians would not know what to make of our contemporary attitudes toward cemeteries and desires to avoid the committal or returning to the cemetery in the future. The early believers were so confident of Jesus' victory over death that from earliest times Christians have called graves "cemeteries," which means, "sleeping places" (Todd W. Van Beck, "Biblical References to the Issue of Funeralization," 62).

These days, some want to avoid the brutal reality of the grave at all costs. Some won't go to the cemetery; others will never go back to a grave, a reality that led to the concept of "perpetual care" sold by cemeteries.

Sometimes the bereaving need a cemetery buddy, especially on the difficult days. Sally Tucker had difficulty visiting her husband's grave. As she approached the fifth anniversary of his death, she asked her friend, Henri Nouwen, to help the children and her "find a new way to visit Bob's grave." On the anniversary, Nouwen arrived at their home with a bouquet of summer flowers. As they sat on the grave, Nouwen dug a hole for the flowers. Then he asked Sally and her son, Mitchell, for stories about Bob.

"At first it seemed really strange to be talking this way, but Henri was so at home that pretty soon Mitchell was telling stories he could remember about his dad," Sally said.

"Henri told us that families in South America go together to visit the grave of a loved one. Sometimes they bring a meal to share and celebrate the life of their loved one. At first this seemed odd, but we came to be able to share an occasional meal at Bob's grave.

"Sometimes Mitch brings his guitar and plays from his heart. Whatever happens, we just sit together with our thoughts" (Sally Tucker, in *Befriending Life*, 120).

Henri paved the way for this family to "reframe" the cemetery into a safe place. The bereaving may face a quandary. Some, quite candidly, don't want to go to the cemetery. Some have been told, "He's not there! So why go?"

Often when I was home, my mother would say, "Could we go by the cemetery?" She didn't like to go alone. There may be some you know who don't like to go alone; as a grief sharer, "tag" along.

It's hard to believe that visiting cemeteries was once a normal expectation. Given our mobility, some adults live many miles from a particular cemetery (even halfway across the country). Some bereaving no longer drive. Some simply want to know that the grave is tidy or that it holds fresh flowers or an arrangement on special days.

Admittedly, a visit to the cemetery will not comfort everyone; for some it is essential in the healing process. In *Befriending Life*, Sally Tucker says, "When we go to the cemetery now, there are still feelings of loss, of what would or could have been, but there is also a deep sense of gratitude for a life lived, for a man who was kind and gentle, and who is still a presence felt in our lives" (121).

....

Blessed are the helpers who are not afraid of cemeteries.

WISE WORDS FOR LOANING

"If we refuse to abide in our pain and *anxiously deny our* pain or move on to control our pain, we preempt God's moving, eliminating the space in which God might minister to us."

—Walter Brueggemann

CHAPTER 19

Recognize
Anniversary Grief

Anniversary: *The annual recurrence
of a date marking a notable event.*

....

*In love we remember those who no longer walk this earth. We
are grateful to God for the gift of their lives, for the joys we
shared, and for the cherished memories that never fade. May
God grant those who mourn the strength to see beyond their
sorrow, sustaining them despite their grief. May the faith that
binds us to our loved ones be a continuing source of comfort.*

—Rabbinical Assembly,
Siddur Sim Shalom for Shabbat and Festivals, 184

Ask a child how old he or she is. Younger children take great delight in reporting, "I'm four *and a half!*" They also have a good idea of when they'll be a year older. Dates are important to children just as anniversaries are important to couples.

Dates are also important to the bereaving. I doubt anyone will forget September 11, 2001. As one young woman said, "It's the day I lost my innocence."

For some who have lost both parents, the death of the second parent is the day they become part of "the older generation" in a family.

In our "move on" culture, some grief sharers miss great opportunities for ministry by failing to note the anniversary.

Grief sharers anticipate anniversaries and the natural occasions for the "anniversary blues." It does not have to be the actual anniversary of the death; some, for example, celebrate a child's birthday instead.

What can you do as a grief sharer?

Ask the bereaving how they intend to deal with the anniversary.

Urge them to do something to "specialize" the day. That may be making time to remember or visiting the cemetery.

Urge them to symbolize the anniversary. They might recognize the anniversary by lighting a candle.

You may open a door to a memory by giving them a candle.

Send flowers or a card. You can let them know you remember by sending a card or calling, or by sending a flower or a small symbolic gift.

Give permission to recognize this anniversary. Your permission could make a difference on a tough day with words like these: "Recognizing that this day is very special for you. Thinking of you today."

As a helper, your noticing may be more appreciated when one spouse or family member wants to forget. This was the case when Lynn's son died. She remembers on the anniversary of his death, "My husband never said a word. Finally, in bed he said, 'Brian's been dead a year. I don't want to ever hear his name again.' I would have gone crazy if it had not been for my good friend Meredith. I can always expect a card or a call with these words: 'Thinking of you today.'"

....

Blessed are the helpers who remember anniversaries.

CHAPTER 20

OBSERVE
MEMORIAL DAY

In my family, Memorial Day weekend means it's time to plant the annuals and wash the porch. It's the traditional start of summer, when bicycles get pulled out of the garage and everyone tries to squeeze into last year's bathing suit. . . . On Memorial Day, several dozen members of my extended family gather at a park near my rural hometown in upstate New York to eat barbecued chicken and deviled eggs. . . . But for us the best thing about the holiday is the part that has become an afterthought for many people—the remembering.

—Amy Dickinson, "Family Legends," 103

In the future, when your son asks you,
"What is the meaning . . . ?" tell him.

—Deut. 6:20-21

The day was difficult for the two little girls to understand. They would ride in the car 90 miles to a tiny cemetery where their grandparents were buried. It wasn't the visit to the graveyard that excited the sisters. It was getting to eat out. These annual pilgrimages lasted until the college years when Melanie Gray decided Decoration Day was merely the first day of summer.

Then Melanie's mother died. Memorial Day was resymbolized. "Now it's very important to get back to Nebraska on or before Memorial Day to decorate her grave." Melanie, like many of us, had to "learn" to appreciate Memorial Day.

Don't just celebrate the day—honor the memory. Memorial Day evolved out of the custom called Decoration Day when families decorated the graves of veterans. N. Patrick Murray urges, "On Memorial Day in America many people go to grave sites to pause and remember, but few sit around the grave and speak of their connection to the one they are honoring, allowing the memories to be plumbed from the depths" (*Living Beyond Your Losses*, 41).

Ask the bereaving about their plans. The first year some may need a "buddy" to accompany them, especially if family members are scattered to the four winds or do not want to go.

Invite the bereaving to lunch or invite them to spend part of the day with cially if it's their first Memorial Day. Or invite them for dessert and conversation.

Encourage the bereaving to honor rather than ignore the day. In "Holidays Without Mom," Melissa Gabbert recommends, "Seize every opportunity to honor the spirit of your loved one" (F3).

....

Blessed are the helpers who celebrate Memorial Day.

WISE WORDS FOR LOANING
"Remembering the person I have loved allows me to slowly heal.
Healing does not mean I will forget. Actually, it means
I will remember. Gently, I will move forward,
never forgetting my past."
—Alan Wolfelt, 47

CHAPTER 21

NOTICE THE CHILDREN

Children old enough to love are old enough to grieve.

—*A Guide to Funeral Planning at*
Saint Francis Xavier Church, 4

Children have minds. They have imaginations.
If they are told the truth in a loving and caring way,
and if they are allowed to express their grief,
they are capable of accepting even the most painful
and devastating losses that life has to offer.

—Helen Fitzgerald, *The Grieving Child*, 193-94

Little children were brought to Jesus for him to place
his hands on them and pray for them.

—Matt. 19:13

Santas in department stores are supposed to be ready for anything.

One Christmas season a young girl climbed onto Santa's lap. Santa launched his litany—"So what do you want Santa to bring you?"

"A house with a mommy and a daddy."

"What else do you want?"

"And a swing on the porch."

In an electronic age, these were a bit unusual. Santa continued: "Have you been a good girl?"

"Uh-huh."

"Have you helped Momma around the house?"

"My momma died."

That day Santa Claus did not know what to say. If Santa Claus does not know what to say, there will be times that a grief sharer doesn't know what to say either.

Some children are unable to comprehend the finality of death. Children do understand, however, that their environment has changed. Unfortunately, funeral rituals are generally adult-oriented events. In the confusion and emotional chaos, children are overlooked. We rationalize that reality by saying, "Oh, children are so resilient." Really?

When possible, take a moment and kneel down to the child's level. Look at the child. Call the child by name. And listen to the child.

Offer to help with the children. Children don't grieve continuously; in fact, you may think their running and playing are inappropriate. Children grieve in segments. In time, they'll come back to their grief. Ask if you may watch them for a while.

Listen. Children may disclose something they've been reluctant to say to a parent because they don't want to increase their distress. Every grieving child deserves adult attention and respect.

Color and draw. Children are continuously taking in data. Since their grief vocabulary is limited, offering crayons and sheets of paper may be an effective way to find out what's on a child's mind and heart.

Kreitemeyer and Heiney identify three goals for sharing grief with children:

Allow the child to put the event(s) into perspective.

Allow the child to make sense of the confusion.

Help the child begin to develop an understanding about death ("Storytelling as a Therapeutic Technique in Group for School-age Oncology Patients," 14-20).

You can aid children in the following ways:

- Avoid euphemism. If you say, "We *lost* your grandmother," the child may respond, "Then let's go look for her." Use simple, direct language. "Your grandmother *died*."

- Give permission to a child's natural curiosity, showing him or her whenever possible.
- Look at the child as you listen.
- Reassure the child.
- Make certain the child understands the death was not his or her fault.
- Encourage familiar routines, such as mealtime and bedtimes.
- Offer hospitality to the child's questions—especially the ones you cannot answer.
- Share a copy of *What Does That Mean? A dictionary of death, dying and grief terms for grieving children and those who love them* by Harold Ivan Smith and Joy Johnson.
- Remember to send cards to the children.

At times after a death, people make promises, especially to children. "If you offer to help children, mean it," Lynn Kelly advises in *Don't Ask for the Dead Man's Golf Clubs.* "After my husband died, every guy that came over told my son he would take him fishing. It never happened, and he never forgot" (14).

Before making a promise to any griever, especially a child, carefully evaluate your ability to follow through. If necessary, qualify your promise with "If I possibly can."

....

Blessed are the helpers who notice children.

CHAPTER 22

GIVE YOUR GRIEF
A VOICE

Society often presses a griever to hold private his or her grief reaction in order not to trouble or disturb others by bringing it out into the open or expressing it in certain ways.

—Charles Corr, "Disenfranchising the Concept
of Disenfranchised Grief," 8

Grieving, close friends may not even recognize their emotional reactions for what they are—
grief needing to be honored!

—Fred Sklar, "Grief as a Family Affair," 109

Let us not become weary in doing good.

—Gal. 6:9

"Never mind me—what about you? What can I do for *you?*" are common words of denial among grief sharers. Sometimes competitive grief care breaks out—to see who can do the most for the family or individual. It's possible to stay so busy "doing" for the bereaving that you never make—or take—time to do your own grief work.

Paying attention to your own needs is not selfish but wise. Who recognizes your need as a grief sharer to grieve? Who offers you support? Despite the increasing appreciation of friendship, many grieving friends feel unacknowledged. What recognition can "only a friend" of the deceased expect? Historically, societal norms mandated that a friend's grief not compete with or interrupt the family's grief (Fred Sklar, "Grief as a Family Affair," 109).

Unfortunately, this expectation encourages friends to discount their own grief to concentrate on the family's needs. Such self-disenfranchisement complicates reconciliation with the death.

Rev. Ron DelBene has conducted hundreds of funerals. Yet the death of his close friend Taylor gave him new insight into grief.

Taylor's death consumed me with grief. I cried. I questioned. At first I could not think beyond myself and my own pain. But then I began to feel guilty for being so self-absorbed. After all, Taylor's wife and children had lost even more than I had.

At the funeral, Taylor's family had the support of the grieving family, which was as it should have been. But because Taylor had meant so much to me, I wanted people to tell me that they were sorry about my loss too. I wanted to be comforted and consoled ("From the Heart," 29).

DelBene describes a sensitive grief sharer's gift of a hug: "At the graveside, one of my clergy friends came up and put his arms around me.

"'You and Taylor were good friends, weren't you?' he said.

"'Yes,' I replied. 'We were.' That was all it took. . . . sobs came from the depths of my heart" (29-30).

Friends may stay so busy supporting the family that they ignore their own grief or the grief of other friends. People will remark, "They are so lucky to have someone like you." The "gotta be strong for the family" mode is believed the appropriate response to a friend's death.

....

Blessed are the grief sharers who give their grief a voice.

....

An old, old friend of my dad's came by. He couldn't talk.
He just put his hand to his heart and gave me a hug.
That was all he needed to do.

—Gary Massaro in Lynn Kelly's, *Don't Ask for the Dead Man's Golf Clubs*, 12

Remember— Grief Sharing is Kingdom Work

*It is a rare and distinctive privilege of ministry
to be welcomed into the small, quiet, broken circle
of the family in such critical times.*

—Thomas C. Oden, *Pastoral Theology*, 294

*Immediately after such a tragedy, and even months later,
people must come to your rescue, people who only want to
hold your hand, not to quote anybody or even say anything,
people who simply bring food and flowers—the basics of
beauty and life—people who sign letters simply,
"Your brokenhearted friend."*

—Dennis Apple, "Consoling a Friend During Tragedy," 7A

*Who knows but that you have come to royal position
for such a time as this?*

—Esther 4:14

Mordecai's words to Esther recorded in Esther 4:14 have long haunted me. As much as I have felt at times empowered by them, I cannot ignore the fact that they follow a sober warning: "If you remain silent at this time" (v. 14). If you fail to respond compassionately and share this grief . . .

This is not just "Well, if you can" work but essential kingdom servanthood. It's an opportunity to partner with God in fulfilling a beatitude—"Blessed are those who mourn," for they will be comforted by God through people like you.

Dwight D. and Mamie Eisenhower both were changed when their three-year-old Ikky died. Eisenhower's biographer, Geoffrey Perret, said, "He had never stopped grieving over Ikky, and never would. There wasn't any readier access to Eisenhower's inner life than through his devastating sense of loss" (*Eisenhower*, 350).

Some grievers come, like Nicodemus, at night, when others are not around—with questions well rehearsed in their "cisterns." On several occasions President Eisenhower played golf with Billy Graham. His need for grief care and his belief that Graham could be trusted led the president to quiz the evangelist about eternal life.

In a moment of grief sharing, Graham assured the president that he believed Jesus' promises without reservation. Eisenhower's biographer comments, "The terrors of death were undoubtedly assuaged for Eisenhower by the prospect of being reunited with Ikky and Ida [the president's mother]" (603).

Graham was criticized for playing golf when the world needed evangelism. But he knew that grief sharing may be part of evangelism—bringing good news into the dark spaces created by grief.

For 18 holes of golf, Graham shared Ike's grief. The conversations did not come in one of Eisenhower's early talks with Graham, but only after the two had developed a relationship.

Grief sharers know that "reachable" moments come in all sorts of settings.

Thomas Oden warns, "The times of approaching death and bereavement are exceptional opportunities for spiritual growth. Sensitive care is required to nurture them toward their fullest potentiality and not let them become an occasion for stumbling. They have great potentiality for demonic as well as creative growth" (*Pastoral Theology*, 297).

Nowhere is this more evident than in the life of Joseph Scriven, who wrote "What a Friend We Have in Jesus."

Twice he experienced excruciating tragedy. In England his bride-to-be drowned the night before their wedding. A few years later, after he moved to

Canada, his fiancé Eliza Roche died suddenly. In his grief, he composed words that have comforted so many:

> *What a Friend we have in Jesus,*
> *All our sins and griefs to bear!*
> *What a privilege to carry*
> *Ev'rything to God in prayer!*
> *O what peace we often forfeit,*
> *O what needless pain we bear,*
> *All because we do not carry*
> *Ev'rything to God in prayer!*

Lyrics of the third verse point to a distress that was not addressed by friends and neighbors in his small rural community before Scriven died from what no one was sure was an accident or suicide:

> *Are we weak and heavy laden,*
> *Cumbered with a load of care?*
> *Precious Savior, still our Refuge!*
> *Take it to the Lord in prayer.*
> *Do thy friends despise, forsake thee?*
> *Take it to the Lord in prayer.*
> *In His arms He'll take and shield thee;*
> *Thou wilt find a solace there.*

Were the words "Do thy friends despise, forsake thee?" a sobering reality as neighbors and friends tired of Scriven's grief? Did he fail to "move on" and "get over it"? The citizens of Port Hope, Ontario, eventually built a monument to honor him. But if friends had been more attentive, more caring, perhaps there would have been no need for a monument.

That griever you have been "meaning" to call or visit may be the next Joseph Scriven. Will a great song, or the equivalent gift—or the grief—be the last line on that person's spiritual résumé?

We are called. We can be equipped. We can, through the power of the Comforter, make a difference in the lives of the bereaving.

When you surrender your need to fix,
your sharing can make a difference to a griever.
When you surrender your need to cure,
your sharing can make a difference to a griever.
When you surrender your timing,
your sharing can make a difference to a griever.
When you surrender all your expectations,
your sharing can make a difference to a griever.
When you care in the Spirit of the Father,
your sharing can make a difference to a griever.

In the ordinary and at times extraordinary "deeds of love and kindness," grief sharing is communicated. Grief sharers often work incognito. I'm moved by one recipient's words: "When I was going through a very difficult time, someone called up and played piano music on my answering machine. It made me feel very loved, and I never discovered who did it" (Editors of Conari Press, *Random Acts of Kindness*, 66).

You as a grief sharer can make a difference.

....

Blessed are the helpers who remember that grief sharing is vital Kingdom work.

WISE WORDS FOR LOANING
"The only way through grief is through it. There are no shortcuts, no detours."
—Patti Reagan Davis

Something happens when we listen
not just with our ears
but with our eyes.
Something happens when we wait out
a griever's words.
Something happens when we express our care
in calming ways.
Something happens
when we keep our promises
even when less than convenient.
Something happens when we pay attention
to the questions of a griever
rather than offer a cheap answer.
Something happens when hearts touch.
Something happens when we remember
Jesus' promise
"Where two or three are gathered . . .
there I will be, too."

Something happens when a caregiver
becomes a grief sharer.

—Harold Ivan Smith

WISE WORDS FOR LOANING

"When all we are and everything we do are called into question,
grant us dignity and direction, grant us patience."

—*A New Zealand Prayer Book*, 583

BIBLIOGraPHY

A New Zealand Prayer Book. San Francisco: HarperSan Francisco, 1997.

Albacete, Lorenzo. "Good Grief and Bad." *New York Times Mag-
azine,* August 27, 2000, sec. 6, 22.

Alexander, Victoria. *Words I Never Thought to Speak: Stories
of Life in the Wake of Suicide.* New York: Lexington Books,
1991.

Anderson, Megory. *Sacred Dying: Creating Rituals for Embracing the End of Life.* Roseville, CA: Prima Publishing, 2001.

Apple, Dennis. "Consoling a Friend During Tragedy." *Olathe
[Kansas] Daily News,* February 1, 1992, 7A.

Attig, Thomas. *The Heart of Grief: Death and the Search for Lasting Love.* New York: Oxford University Press, 2000.

Bartlett, John. *Familiar Quotations: A Collection of Passages,
Phrases and Proverbs Traced to Their Sources in Ancient and
Modern Literature.* 1855. 15th ed: Emily Morison Beck, ed.
Boston: Little, Brown and Company, 1980.

Bass, Dorothy C. *Receiving the Day: Christian Practices for
Opening the Gift of Time.* San Francisco: Jossey-Bass, 2000.

Benson, Robert. *Living Prayer.* New York: Tarcher/Putnam,
1998.

Bonhoeffer, Dietrich. *Life Together.* Trans. John W. Doberstein.
New York: Harper and Row, 1954.

Broxterman, Peggy, whose son died in the Oklahoma City bomb-
ing. Cited in "Perspectives." *Newsweek,* May 7, 2001.

Brueggemann, Walter, with Frost, Steve. *Psalmist's Cry: Scripts
for Embracing Lament.* Kansas City: The House Studio,
2010, 42.

Bush, George W. Washington National Cathedral "Bush's
Speech." *Kansas City Star,* September 15, 2001, A12.

Caldwell, Charmaine, Marsha McGee, and Charles Pryor. "The

Sympathy Card as Cultural Assessment of American Attitude Toward Death, Bereavement and Extending Sympathy: A Replicated Study." *Omega* 37(2) (1998).

Chaffin, Kenneth. "From the Front Porch." *Family Ministry* 14:3 (fall 2000.

Chittister, Joan. Lecture, Country Club Christian Church, Kansas City, Missouri. November 9, 2009.

Claypool, John R. *God the Ingenious Alchemist; Transforming Tragedy into Blessing.* Harrisburg, PA: Morehouse, 2006, 40.

Close, Henry T. "A Funeral Service." *Voices* 1 (1969).

Corr, Charles A. "Disenfranchising the Concept of Disenfranchised Grief." *Omega* 38:1 (1998-99).

Daniels, Susan. "Wirthlin Study Tracks Consumer Attitude Trends." *The Director,* 68:2 (February 1996).

David, Lester, and Irene David. *Ike and Mamie: The Story of the General and His Lady.* New York: G. P. Putnam's Sons, 1981.

Davis, Patti. *The Long Goodbye.* New York: Knopf, 2004, np.

DelBene, Ron, with Mary Montgomery and Herb Montgomery. *From the Heart.* Nashville: Upper Room Books, 1991.

Dickinson, Amy. "Family Legends." *Time,* May 31, 1999.

Dravecky, David, and Jan Dravecky, with Ken Gire. *When You Can't Come Back: A Story of Courage and Grace.* Grand Rapids: Zondervan Publishing House, 1992.

Edelman, Hope. *Motherless Daughters: The Legacy of Loss.* New York: Delta, 1994.

Editors of Conari Press. *Random Acts of Kindness.* Berkeley, CA: Conari Press, 1993.

Euster, Gerald L. "Memorial Contributions: Remembering the Elderly Deceased and Supporting the Bereaved." *Omega* 23:3 (1991).

Farmer, Patrick J. "Bereavement Counseling." *Journal of Pastoral Counseling* 15(2) (1980).

Fifth-grade Class of Westwood Elementary School. "As We See It: Grateful for the Big and Small in Life." *Kansas City Star,*

November 20,2000, C20.

Fitzgerald, Helen. *The Grieving Child: A Parent's Guide.* New York: Fireside Press, 1992.

Ford, Michael. *Father Mychal Judge: An Authentic American Hero.* New York: Paulist Press, 2002, 203.

Fulgham, Kathie Scobee. "Challenger Daughter Offers Reassuring Words." *Atlanta Journal-Constitution,* September 30, 21001, E15.

Gabbert, Melissa. "Holidays Without Mom." *Kansas City Star,* December 15, 1999, F3.

Gaidies, Martha. "The Columbine Tragedy: Part III: The Search for Understanding and Healing in the Wake of Tragedy." *The Director* 71:7 (July 1999), 54.

Goodman, Ellen. "Mourning Gets the Bum's Rush." *Kansas City Star,* August 2, 1998, B7.

Grabowski, Jo-Anne, and Thomas T. Frantz. "Latinos and Anglos: Cultural Experiences of Grief Intensity." *Omega* 26:4 (1993).

Gray, Melanie. "Ready to Remember." *Kansas City Star,* May 24, 1997, G3.

Grollman, Earl A., ed. *Concerning Death: A Practical Guide for the Living.* Boston: Beacon Press, 1974.

Grossman, Cathy Lynn. (2008 22 September). Rabbi Wolpe's "faith" takes on atheists and fanatics alike. *USA Today, electronic version.*

Harris, Helen Wilson. "Congregational Care for the Chronically Ill, Dying and Bereaved." *Family Ministry* 14:1 (2000).

Higgins, Tim. "Virginia Greenlease, Benefactor of Rockhurst Schools, Is Dead at 91." *Kansas City Star,* September 25, 2001, B1.

Huntley, Theresa. *When Your Child Dies.* Minneapolis: Augsburg Press, 2001.

_____. *When Your Child Loses a Loved One.* Minneapolis: Augsburg Press, 2001.

Kelly, Lynn. *Don't Ask for the Dead Man's Golf Clubs: Advice for Friends When Someone Dies.* Littleton, CO: Kelly Communications, 2000.

King, Martin Luther, Jr. Cited in Zelizer, Gerald K. "King, Rabbi Expose What New Age Religion Lacks." *USA Today,* January 18, 1998, 13A.

Kushner, Harold S. *Living a Life That Matters: Resolving the Conflict Between Conscience and Success.* New York: Knopf, 2001.

Lobel, Arnold. *Days with Frog and Toad.* New York: HarperCollins, 1979.

Lunn, Carolyn. *Joy—anyway!* Kansas City: Beacon Hill Press, 1992.

Lynch, Thomas. "A Serious Undertaking." *The American Funeral Director,* September 2001.

_____. *The Undertaking: Life Studies from the Dismal Trade.* New York: Norton, 1997.

Manning, Doug. *Don't Take My Grief Away from Me.* San Francisco: Harper and Row, 1979.

_____. *The Funeral: A Chance to Touch, a Chance to Serve, a Chance to Heal.* Oklahoma City, OK: In-Sight Books, 2001.

Mastlin, Simeon J., ed. *Gates of Mitzvah: A Guide to the Jewish Life Cycle.* New York: Central Conference of American Rabbis, 1979.

Miller, James E., with Susan C. Cutshall. *The Art of Being a Healing Presence: A Guide for Those in Caring Relationship.* Fort Wayne, IN: Willowgreen, 2001.

Murray, N. Patrick. *Living Beyond Your Losses: The Healing Journey Through Grief.* Harrisburg, PA: Morehouse, 1994.

Nouwen, Henri. *In Memoriam.* Notre Dame, IN: Ava Maria Press, 1980, Quote 19.

Oden, Thomas C. *Pastoral Theology: Essentials of Ministry.* San Francisco: Harper and Row, 1983.

Patterson, Ronald M. "The Positive Power of Doubt." *Faith at Work,* fall 2000.

Perret, Geoffrey. *Eisenhower.* New York: Random House, 1999.

Pohl, Christine D. *Making Room: Recovering Hospitality as a Christian Tradition.* Grand Rapids: William B. Erdmann's Publishing Company, 1999.

Porter, Beth, ed. *Befriending Life: Encounters with Henri Nouwen.* New York: Doubleday, 2001.

Porter, Jerry D. "Commission: Saints Suffer Too." *Holiness Today,* August 2001.

Putnam, Robert D. *Bowling Alone: The Collapse and Revival of American Community.* New York: Simon and Schuster, 2000.

Rabbinical Assembly. *Siddur Sim Shalom for Shabbat and Festivals.* N.p.: The United Synagogue of Conservative Judaism, 1998.

Richman, Linda. *I'd Rather Laugh: How to Be Happy When Life Has Other Plans for You.* New York: Warner Press, 2001.

Rivers, Joan. *Bouncing Back: I've Survived Everything . . . and I Mean Everything . . . and You Can, Too.* New York: HarperCollins, 1997.

Roberts, Barbara (cite). *Death Without Denial.* Troutdale, OR: NewSage Press, 78.

Rohr, Richard. *Everything Belongs: The Gift of Contemplative Prayer.* New York: Crossroad, 2000.

Rosten, Leo. *Leo Rosten's Treasury of Jewish Quotations.* New York: Bantam Books, 1980.

Rupp, Joyce. *The Cup of Our Life: A Guide for Spiritual Growth.* Notre Dame, IN: Ave Maria Press, 1997.

_____. *Praying Our Goodbyes.* Notre Dame, IN: Ave Maria Press, 1988.

Russell, Brent. "Joseph of Arimathaea: The Patron Saint of Funeral Directors." *The Director,* October 1996.

Russell, Jan Jarboe. *Lady Bird: A Biography of Mrs. Johnson.* New York: Scribner, 1999.

Saint Francis Church. *A Guide to Funeral Planning at Saint Francis Xavier Church.* Kansas City: Saint Francis Xavier

Church, fall 1996.

Seaver, George. *David Livingstone: His Life and Letters.* New York: Harper and Brothers, 1957.

Shneidman, Edwin S. Suicidology and the University: A founder's Reflections at 80, *Suicide & Life Threatening Behavior, 2l(1),* 1.

Sittser, Gerald L. *A Grace Disguised: How the Soul Grows Through Loss.* Grand Rapids: Zondervan Publishing House, 1995.

Sklar, Fred. "Grief as a Family Affair: Property Rights, Grief Rights, and the Exclusion of Close Friends as Survivors." *Omega* 24:2 (1991-92).

Sklar, Fred, and Shirley F. Hartley. "Close Friends as Survivors: Bereavement Patterns in a 'Hidden' Population." *Omega* 21:2 (1990), 103.

Smedes, Lewis B. *Choices: Making Right Decisions in a Complex World.* San Francisco: Harper & Row, 1986, 32.

Smith, Harold Ivan, and Johnson, Joy. *What Does That Mean? A dictionary of death, dying and grief terms for grieving children and those who love them.* Omaha, NE: Centering.

Unruh, David. "Death and Personal History: Strategies of Identity Preservation." *Social Problems* 30:3 (1983).

Van Beck, Todd W. "R. Newman: Sexton and Undertaker, Old NorthChurch, Boston." *The Director,* January 1998, 46-47.

_____. "Biblical References to the Issue of Funeralization." *The American Funeral Director,* May 2000.

_____. "The Fossores: Our Early Funeral Directors and Cemeterians. Funerals in the Bible." *The American Funeral Director,* March 2000, 60-61.

Wagner, Lois. Cited in Palmer, Anna. Writing the Last Chapter: PLNU School of Nursing professor advises tackling end-of-life issues now. *Viewpoint,* Summer 2005, 3-5.

Wilcock, Penelope. *Spiritual Care of Dying and Bereaved People.* Harrisburg, PA: Morehouse, 1996.

Wiltshire, Susan Ford. *Season of Grief and Grace.* Nashville:

Vanderbilt University Press, 1994, 145.

Wolfelt, Alan D. "Companioning Versus Treating: Beyond the Medical Model of Bereavement Caregiving: Part 3." *The Forum,* 24:6 (November-December 1998).

_____. *Creating Meaningful Funeral Ceremonies: A Guide for Caregivers.* Ft. Collins, CO: Companion Press, 1994.

_____. "Helping a Friend in Grief." *Thanatos,* winter 1990.

_____. "Understanding Grief: Helping Yourself Heal." Presentation in Olathe, KS, February 11, 1999.

Wolpe, David. Cited in Grossman, Cathy Lynn. Rabbi Wolpe's "faith" takes on atheists and fanatics alike. *USA Today,* September 22, 2008, *electronic version.*

Worden, J. William. *Grief Counseling and Grief Therapy: A Handbook for the Mental Health Practitioner.* 2nd ed. New York: Spring, 1991.

ABOUT THE AUTHOR

Harold Ivan Smith is a thanatologist on the teaching faculties of Saint Luke's Hospital, Kansas City, Missouri, and the Carondolet Medical Institute in Eau Claire, Wisconsin.

He is recognized as a Fellow in Thanatology by the Association for Death Education and Counseling. He has also received the Distinguished Service Award from ADEC in 2009. He has served as Co-Chair of the ADEC Conferences in Albuquerque in 2005 and Kansas City in 2010.

He earned the doctorate from Asbury Theological Seminary and the EdS. from George Peabody College of Vanderbilt University.

He speaks frequently to grievers and grief counselors and educators. He has lectured in Vietnam, Taiwan, Switzerland, England, and Haiti.

His writing has been published in *Illness, Loss, and Crisis, Living with Loss, The Director, The Forum,* and other magazines.

His primary research is on borrowing grief narratives from the U.S. Presidents and First Ladies.

He has facilitated Grief Gatherings, creative storytelling groups for grievers, at Saint Luke's Hospital, Kansas City, Missouri, for 16 years.

Harold Ivan Smith
P.O. Box 24688
Kansas City, MO 64131
816-444-5301
friendgrief@mindspring.com